POETRY ESCAPE

POEMS FROM THE MIDLANDS

Edited By Elle Berry

First published in Great Britain in 2019 by:

YoungWriters®
Est. 1991

Young Writers
Remus House
Coltsfoot Drive
Peterborough
PE2 9BF
Telephone: 01733 890066
Website: www.youngwriters.co.uk

All Rights Reserved
Book Design by Ashley Janson
© Copyright Contributors 2019
SB ISBN 978-1-78988-194-3
Printed and bound in the UK by BookPrintingUK
Website: www.bookprintinguk.com
YB0393T

FOREWORD

Since 1991 our aim here at Young Writers has been to encourage creativity in children and young adults and to inspire a love of the written word. Each competition is tailored to the relevant age group, hopefully giving each student the inspiration and incentive to create their own piece of creative writing, whether it's a poem or a short story. We truly believe that seeing their work in print gives students a sense of achievement and pride.

For our latest competition Poetry Escape, we challenged secondary school students to free their creativity and escape the maze of their minds using poetic techniques as their tools of navigation. They had several pathways to choose from, with each one offering either a specific theme or a writing constraint. Alternatively they could forge their own route, because there's no such thing as a dead end where imagination is concerned.

The result is an inspiring anthology full of ideas, hopes, fears and imagination, proving that creativity really does offer escape, in whatever form you need it.

We encourage young writers to express themselves and address topics that matter to them, which sometimes means exploring sensitive or difficult topics. If you have been affected by any issues raised in this book, details on where to find help can be found at: **www.youngwriters.co.uk/support**.

CONTENTS

Ashby School, Ashby-De-La-Zouch

Tom Harris (17)	1
Matthew Daniel Bedford (17)	3
Dan Hewitt (17)	5
Francesca Morgan (16)	7

Countesthorpe Leysland Community College, Countesthorpe

Emma Broadhead (11)	9

Derby High School, Littleover

Lucy Masterson (12)	10
Elspeth Sibthorp-Quarmby	12

Hollygirt School, Nottingham

Deniz Yuksel (12)	13

Kingsmead School, Hednesford

Luke Garner (11)	14
Katie Clay (11)	16
Danielle Anslow (17)	19
Alfie James (11)	20
Ellie-Mae Perkins (17)	22
Maisie Louise Radford (17)	24
Emily Nelson (14)	25
Scarlett Taylor (12)	26

Littleover Community School, Littleover

Thea Kaur Badh-Drost (11)	27
Aisha Azam (11)	28
Grace Berry (11)	30
Zihan Qin (11)	32
William Wright (11)	34
Sumaira Azam (13)	36
Andrew Rodwell (13)	38
Zoya Ali (11)	39
Henry Smith (12)	40
Tyler Hardwick (12)	42
Zaibaa Tair (12)	43
Shabbir Ali Raja (13)	44
Harleen Dhamrait (12)	46
Sophie Buxton (12)	48
Thomas Fowler (13)	50
Lizzie Bellamy (12)	52
Saba Ashraf (11)	53
Imaan Ali (11)	54
Jack Williams (11)	55
Christy Jince (12)	56
Katie Louise Birks (11)	58
Safiyah Khan (11)	59
Sienna Sagoo (12)	60
Khaira Ahmed (11)	62
Bronwyn Wigley (13)	63
Jacob Curd (11)	64
Mariya Hussain (13)	65
Haider Ali Irfan (13)	66
Huzayfah Shaid (13)	67
Alisha Mahmood (13)	68
Katie House (11)	69
Jazmine Hafez (12)	70
Sonny Rooney (12)	71

Shifa Aziz (12)	72
Naila Mustafa (12)	73
Oliver Young (12)	74
Torsten Ellis (13)	75
Jessica Louise Angel Bird (12)	76
Claudia Holmes (12)	77
Abigail Maia Morgan (11)	78
Megan Hurn (12)	79
Nia Carey Swain (11)	80
Jenny Cameron (12)	81
Evie Kininmonth (12)	82
Tanisha Latif (11)	83

Lutterworth High School, Lutterworth

Alasdair Rowan (12)	84
Grace Ann Harrison (12)	86

Quinton House School, Northampton

Myles Rowley	87

Sir Thomas Boughey Academy, Halmerend

Tessa Smith (12)	88
Hannah Gallimore (11)	90
Oliver Birch (13)	91
Ellie-May Worrall (12)	92
Harry Hulse (12)	93
Damian Wilson (12)	94
Shi Alisha Koroma (13)	95
Isobel Mary Connolly (12)	96
Maddison Rose Pemberton (11)	97
Nakisha Lei Evans (12)	98
Leighton Pugh (13)	99
Oscar James Campbell (12)	100
Gracie Rondel (13)	101
Christopher Babb (11)	102
Jessica Clay (11)	103
Laila Olivia Yates (11)	104
Comfort Sellers (11)	105

Kacey Williams (11)	106
James Nicholas Endall (13)	107
Gabriella Jayne Healey (13)	108
Sophie Grace Jervis (11)	109
Olivia Windsor (13)	110
Alissa-Rose Graham (11)	111
Kian Windsor Finney (13)	112
Crystal Knott (11)	113
Tia Lily Pemberton (12)	114
Joshua Luke Knott (12)	115
Daisy Westwood (12)	116
Millie Reay (12)	117
Calum David Wintle (13)	118

The William Allitt School, Newhall

Matthew Kimberlin (11)	119
Aimee Grace Patrick (14)	120
Chloe Morgan Bradbury (11)	122
Lexi Ross (11)	123
Jacob Paul Ratcliffe (11)	124
Mikey Wilkinson (11)	125
Keeley Wood (11)	126
Erin Marie Satchwell (12)	127
Natalie Ruddle (11)	128
George Spencer (11)	129
Peter Robson (11)	130
Libby Fearn (11)	131
Emily Mae Brookes (11)	132
Franki Sweet (11)	133
Skye Evans-Sellers (11)	134

Tudor Grange Samworth Academy, Leicester

Kia Ann Cooke (13)	135
Hanna Maria Szlaga (13)	136
Ben Lunn (13)	138
Cassidy Katie McKinnon (14)	140
Hassan Ismail	141
Nicol Slizewska-Gniazdowska (13)	142
Alivia Hay	143
Aprinder Kaur (13)	144

Mason Thomas	145
Cristina Maria Jipa (12)	146
Emma Foxon (13)	147
Nicole Szalai	148
Cyrus Marriott (12)	149
Eleanor Chambers (12)	150
Stefani Todorovic	151
Cole Barratt (12)	152
Shay Tramaine Dixon (12)	153
Florentina Denisia Murat (13)	154
Deividas Zemlauskis (12)	155
Abube Calvin Onuchukwu (13)	156
Dylan Wardle	157
Augustine Jakopo-Taylor (12)	158
Ethan Thomas	159
Alexandra Brinzoi (13)	160
Anthony William Shelley (13)	161
Corey Beatty	162
Abbas Jafari (12)	163
Holly Harding	164
Mohammad Ahmadi	165
Cody Watson (13)	166
Chelsey Smullen	167
Kane Donovan (12)	168

Wilsthorpe School, Long Eaton

Amélie Tuck (13)	169
Izzy Johnson (13)	170

THE POEMS

FORTUNE TELLER

Smooth glass and concrete rise skyward
Once bound to simple drawing -
Now an objective reality.

Within the glorious industrial shadow,
the smog, the smoke and blackened light - lie a people in ruin.

Unsolicited loyalty, a scandal,
distance a key,
Highly insular yet terribly true.

Revolution but a dream,
Mechanised symphonies oppress us,
A freedom from choice.

The misdirected wander far
Out across the wastes of what once was,
Searching for something.

Idealistic form, dogmatic nation,
The tyrants rise and fall
But tyranny always stands.

Every crime, capital,
Every capital, a crime.

Society on the peripherals
Fiefdoms of fear.

People screaming for freedom -
and the right of indecision.

The grass is always greener.

We live in a hierarchy of concrete heresy and cement hearts.

Soon, an objective reality.

Tom Harris (17)
Ashby School, Ashby-De-La-Zouch

RORY THE RED NOSE ROVER

My first car and my best friend.
Forever with me, until the end.
Throaty 8 valve sound,
A strong 21-year-old warrior all around.

The best car in the UK.
But the most annoying car in the world, JK!
His bouncy hydragas, full of charm,
You can feel the road through your forearm.

I cannot believe I won the bid,
It must have been fate, I felt like a kid!
I feel the bite on the drive.
Strong and clear, he's alive!

Not quite a manual choke!
Out of the exhaust, you will not find white smoke.
What a car!
Definitely the best, and by far!
The only one in the country, he's very rare.
If you want him, then tough, I don't care!
He's got a new battery too!
Gutsy and British all the way through.

I'd have struggled to find a better first car
But thinking about it, he hits the high bar.

His sills are not looking like the rest of him
Rusted all the way through. I'll have to fill a jar of money to the rim!

Matthew Daniel Bedford (17)
Ashby School, Ashby-De-La-Zouch

THE SHOWER

A corner of something: unbiased comfort?

Judas among men can step foot through this
glass turned to ice and feel at home.
The tall, opaque sheets stand stronger than concrete -
an armoured wall of Roman shields
tight in formation, turned opal by catching light from
across a streamed room.

Slowly the falling of almost invisible, bullets to
a warm, running hug. Holding to you like
a second skin.
Compressing the fast paces of the outside world to
that of a theatre production.
To be examined, rewound and contemplated
upon.

A corner of something: quiet therapy?

The only sounds are that of the droplets that
ricochet off the plastic bed of polymers sewn tight.
Keeping secrets.

A waterfall, cascading over skin like comforting hands,
penetrates and purges emotion out into the tangible.
In this glass shell, a man can be anyone,
feel anything and yet this asylum will not speak it.

In this corner of something, I stand.

Bathed - submerged in my own thoughts.
A monument to a momentary bliss.
Solitude in our crowded, dry lives.

Dan Hewitt (17)
Ashby School, Ashby-De-La-Zouch

BATTLE'S WAKE

The legion of furious grey clouds,
They march against the burnished battleground.
The brooding, stormy armada lay in wait along the horizon.
These branches of the solitary dead man's arms,
Sway in the winter wind.
A barren wasteland of exposed earth stretches as far as the eye can see.
All is silent now,
Except for the jovial song that carries on breath.
"The battle is over now, O' weary traveller,
Yonder by the green.
Lay to rest, weary traveller, though the war is not yet won."
Night falls to rest with the bodies of the fallen,
As silent as the screams of these dead men.

Set sail the billowing armada,
Join your comrades in flight.
Appease the chained, cruel circle of battle.
Join your ever dead men,
Ever dying men in everlasting life.
"O' weary traveller, turn your head and heart, turn away.
Do not fall into the embrace,
Of the devil men's branches.
Cast away their necklace of rope.
Please save yourselves,
Do not join this eternal, brutal fight.

O'er yonder weary traveller, many years distance peace will be found.
Do not climb to the bosom,
Of the needy and the damned.
Await your flight of wit' the heavenly shrouds will carry."

Francesca Morgan (16)
Ashby School, Ashby-De-La-Zouch

IN THE FUTURE

In the future, I would like to be,
As happy as a caterpillar munching joyfully.
In the future, I would like to be,
As successful as a student getting A's daily.
In the future, I would like to see,
Cars flying through the air gracefully.
In the future, I would like to see,
Animals galore, running wildly.
In the future, I would like to know,
How people lived a thousand years ago.
In the future, I would like to know,
How I could meet an ancient pharaoh.
What would you do, if the future, you could see?
What would you stop, what changes would there be?
What would you think, if you knew what happened next?
Would you feel bored, would you feel vexed?
I, for one, would love to know,
In the future, what will come and go?

Emma Broadhead (11)
Countesthorpe Leysland Community College, Countesthorpe

INNER THOUGHTS

Haiku poetry

I am made of war,
Sometimes I'm just not okay
I think you know why.

Hurt me, why don't you?
I am nothing anyway
I'm irrelevant

Bullets fly at me,
Bullets of words to break me
That make me bleed out.

I'm a nobody,
Don't mean anything to you,
That's why you hurt me.

So call me ugly,
Tell me that you think I'm fat.
Perhaps that, I am.

Keep on beating me -
I probably deserve it,
I am not okay.

I used to think that,
Used to think I was no one.
Just because of you.

But now I will rise,
Watch as I become stronger
As your bullets fly.

Because now I know,
Who I am and shall now be,
Is not down to you.

Lucy Masterson (12)
Derby High School, Littleover

IF I COULD FLY I WOULD

If I could fly, I would
But my legs are stuck in the mud
If I were able to sleep
I would stop counting sheep
Everything I would do
I'd still be missing you
You're the one I want
But you are only in the front
My head is clear
When you are not here
My eyes are sharper
My brain, smarter
But I still miss you
If I could fly, I would
But my heart is stuck in the mud.

Elspeth Sibthorp-Quarmby
Derby High School, Littleover

ENVIRONMENT

What has our environment come to?
If only we could change what we have done
The birds, the animals, the plants
All just thrown away
Our oxygen thrown away
Our water polluted, literally
Our animals killed, literally
Our world being destroyed, literally
For no reason
Help the environment!
Help the world!
Help life!

Deniz Yuksel (12)
Hollygirt School, Nottingham

THE MAZE

There I stand, in an unfamiliar place,
With no ordinary people and no familiar face.
All I see are lots of hedges,
Tall and green with pointed edges.
Mist and fog sneak down every trail,
And rain pours down, hail after hail.
I start to feel lost after feeling a haze,
As I suddenly realise that I am in a maze.

I look around me, trying to find a route,
Which would probably take me all the way through.
But not much is seen through all of the rain,
And I start to get tired, my eyes start to strain.
Alas, I find routes, at least four or five,
Yet I need to choose one, so I can survive.
I make up my mind, and enter the maze,
My heart in my mouth and a big worry raised.

Corner after corner, I quicken my pace,
"There's no turning back," I say, like I'm in a race.
Dead ends and thin paths, I make my way,
To get to the end before it reaches day.
Two routes down, and I still have no luck,
And with three left to go, I could actually be stuck.
I choose my third route, hoping this is that path,
But yet again, it isn't, and it costs the time I have.

The fourth, like the rest, is full of traps,
Dead ends, monsters and also false paths.
Some monsters are fearful and put me off course,
And some are half men and some are half horse.
Traps involve courses, sorcery and spells,
Like endless pit holes and unlucky wells.
Illusions are like thunder, fake pathways and more,
There are also fake exits and fake, untouchable walls.

It seems my only escape point is route number five,
But not much time is left for me to survive.
I rush down the route with not much time to spare,
And mysteriously, the route is bare.
There are no monsters or magical traps,
And no dead ends, not even false paths.
I slow down a bit, knowing there is no concern,
But how wrong I am, the worst is yet to come...

It starts to turn day, the sun barely in sight,
Little do I know that I am in for a fright...

Now I see the exit, just about in sight,
But I need to be fast as it nearly isn't night.
Just before I reach the gate, I am now in shock,
Because as it turns out all along, the gate had a lock!
"I was tricked!" I tell myself, engulfed in dismay,
But as soon as I say this, it turns from night to day.
I suddenly realise that is no trick, and now I see the key
But before I can reach it, I'm taken back to reality...

Luke Garner (11)
Kingsmead School, Hednesford

INSECURITY

A poem about inner insecurity

One, get up... I said, *get up!*
You don't want to ruin your reputation!
Well, not that it wasn't ruined already.

Two, pft... get dressed!
Oh, and this time,
maybe *try* and make yourself pretty.
It wouldn't hurt to put effort in...
wimp!

Three, oh... my... gosh...
Get some make-up on!
Your ugliness would blind anyone!
Put plenty of layers on too...
Nobody can see your true colours.

Four, have you seen the time, four eyes?
If you don't move that butt,
you'll be late! The teachers hate you already,
I wouldn't want them to hate you
even more if I were you.

Five, don't be seen by anyone,
You're too ugly to be seen!
Even blind people would be able
to see your ugliness!

Six, you dare talk in this class
and so lord help me, I will make
your life a living hell.
Your high-pitched voice is enough
to break multiple eardrums!

Seven, don't go near that food.
You are fat enough already!
Lord help you if any food entered your system...
you would be the fattest person alive!

Eight, stop concentrating in class
and focus on hoping that the day will end soon!
Nobody cares about your grades anyway.

Nine, grab your bag and go!
Nobody can stand you much longer.
Just get home and
avoid *everyone.*

Ten, take that paint off your face
and remove those 'pretty' clothes...
Ew! Get something on!
Those stretch marks are so gross!

Eleven, get your onesie on...
At least it covered your disgusting
body and features.
Maybe consider staying in there for the rest of your life
It would do the world some good.

Twelve, go to sleep early so tomorrow comes and goes quicker
Oh, and one last thing to remember...

You'll never be pretty, ever!

Katie Clay (11)
Kingsmead School, Hednesford

DEPRESSED RAMBLINGS

When I cry you might not be there.
If I die you couldn't care.
I'm here for you, you are too.
Yet alone into the darkness I stare.

One million spirals, a jumbled-up fate.
One wrong move and hell is bent.
Yet the moves I make are only wrong.
A never-ending wail of the saddest song.

The words I say are true but fall upon a deaf ear.
Yet the speaker is a deaf-mute and heeds none.
And the audience never takes the moral home.

So now lost I am on the most fragile crack
I know I'm broken yet you I still hold.

I hold worry. Nameless, yet woven between it binds.
Slowly. Slowly choking, not done until both of us die.
A blade is needed to escape the soft trap.
We know that few see the danger of the wool used to make the hat.

Now the suffocation continues,
My vision tunnelled and black.
But the light around is present,
An open eye is all it takes to see,
The halo providing an escape available to you and me.

Danielle Anslow (17)
Kingsmead School, Hednesford

THE NIGHT ADVENTURES OF TOMMY BELFRAY

It was all quiet in the house,
You couldn't even hear the scurry of the mouse,
His head was held high,
But he was wishing time would go by,
He sat there, bored,
But dreaming he had a sword,

He then fell fast asleep,
With the warmth of the cosy heat,
He then had one of the wildest dreams,
He had, no one else had seen,
He woke up in a colossal, ancient castle,
Where there was no hassle,
What was he to do?
Go sit on a golden loo?

After he got out of bed,
He got a metal helmet for his head,
Then a young, poor maid came and said,
"How was your sleep in bed?"
There were many fascinating words to describe,
But all he could think of was his scribe.

He set out of the castle,
Where he found a burgundy horse with a bustle

He was so energetic and set,
He said, "I would go on an adventure, I bet."
Over the daunting hill and far away,
He had nothing left to pay,
He then yelled, "I give up!"
Until the young discouraged boy found a special pup,
Which teleported him to a cold, eerie dungeon.

He sat there, melancholy and sullen,
Until footsteps appeared... it was Golem,
Hiding in the corner like a coward,
He felt small and outpowered.

He feared for his life,
While Golem had a sword as sharp as a knife,
He got closer, destroying everything happy,
He only wished for his mummy.

Tears of fear came pouring out,
He was dead, no doubt,
Bang!
He opened his pearly eyes,
Where he'd been was all lies,
He glanced frantically around, it was home,
Peering down was a chocolate gnome,
"At least I ain't dead!" he said,
"Now off I go for a sleep in bed."

Alfie James (11)
Kingsmead School, Hednesford

FREE

One space, of calm and peace;
Where gentle words fall upon deaf ears
Where rain falls
And trees grow over us.
A place of comfort and sincerity
With honest eyes
Which smile under the moon
With warmth in the heart.

One space, of tears and tingles;
Where warmth falls from one honest eyes
And pain grows in the place of smiles
Where hearts race
And no one can find an escape
With withered hope
With aches in every breath
In every little tick or swish
Where nothing can stop those words,
The ones that build in the back -
In the back on the mind,
Until they take over,
The abuse they find,
Strips of all composure.

One space, of stars and laughs;
Where the sweet mind spends their hours

Where orange grows
And small, white specks settle on the grass
A place of steadiness
With the occasional pass of a car
Which signals time to rest.

One space, which holds the key
To finally,
Being free.

Ellie-Mae Perkins (17)
Kingsmead School, Hednesford

MY GRANDFATHER LAUGHS FOR ONLY HER

Song of fairy tales, sung out of reach,
Circle the tree trunk, mushroom ring.
Affection exceeds you, you've taken all mine,
And left me with none, oh marauder divine.
A proposal of wealth, happily ever after,
Recoil; remember the still point and falter.

Dance for me when you're out of reach,
So your enchantment may not burn my sandpaper hands.
Ring me with laughter, halo my heart,
My jealous desire to feel that too.
Lessons not forgotten, scorn welded cage,
Afraid that our harmonies shall never sing as one.

Don't - under the moon-drunk stars.
Don't - under the broken sun.
Don't - under the crippled day.
Don't - mumbles the obelisk son.

The youthful chains that encircled me are perished,
But your bonds upon my life have me writhing.
My shoulders shake, an ageless heart aglow,
Shame; the painful light escapes from below.

Maisie Louise Radford (17)
Kingsmead School, Hednesford

ADVENTURES ARE SO FUN

Adventures are so fun
especially in the sun
enthusiastically exploring about
feel free to laugh and shout
losing myself in nature
it's getting a little bit later
Wind shakes the trees
and also takes the leaves
it's dark now in the woods
I need to use my hood
Rain comes flying down
making piles of mud all around.

Adventures are so fun
Especially in the sun.

Emily Nelson (14)
Kingsmead School, Hednesford

DINNER WITH CROCODILES

What a funny word,
It means different things,
To the biggest nerd,
To a pig with wings.
It can go from writing with a pen,
Or dinner with a curious crocodile,
And running with a hyper hen,
It might take a while.
But it will be worth it in the end,
Because after all, good adventure,
I would recommend.

Scarlett Taylor (12)
Kingsmead School, Hednesford

I DID SOMETHING TERRIBLE EARLIER

I did something terrible earlier,
Something unforgivable.
Every minute of the day my heart is beating scarcely.
The noises around me are tuning out and all that I can hear are the footsteps of people passing by in the school hallways.
I am waiting through the lessons, each minute getting slower.
I am trying to hold in the tears as I don't want to draw attention to myself.
Every time the door opens a horrible shiver runs down my spine,
I can smell the fear sticking to me like a magnet,
I can taste the guilt lying on my tongue,
I am trapped within the walls of my school,
I know what's about to happen,
I can see the headmaster at the door, ready to turn the handle,
I am feeling deep regret.
All my biggest fears are coming true.
At that moment, my heart is dropping, and I can feel a tsunami of cold,
wet tears rushing down my cheeks.

Thea Kaur Badh-Drost (11)
Littleover Community School, Littleover

WARNING ON WARMING

The exquisite round sun, excelled brightly up high,
We all know that autumn is nigh.
So we cherish the days we have left in the sun,
Running and skipping - having all sorts of fun!

Now winter is here, we cuddle up snug,
I have in my hand, a hot chocolate mug.
We await the cool, winter breeze, that chills to the bone,
But the sun is still high, the rain all alone.

I look out the window - rest my mug on the pane,
I stare for hours, where on Earth are snow and rain?
It was now Christmas and not a single sign of cold,
It was global warming, I had been told.

Polar bears were extinct, snow leopards rare,
I'd also heard the reservoirs were bare.
Oh, what would we do without any water?
And the percentage of sea life growing larger and larger.

There is no water left - it's extremely hot,
We're all thirsty - and we haven't forgot
All those people that gave us warning,
And now we believe them, as we are mourning.

It turned out to be true,
Now we apologise.

But there's nothing we can do,
We should've opened our eyes!

Two weeks have passed now and *still* not one speck of snow,
Imagine not being able to see its mystical glow.

Aisha Azam (11)
Littleover Community School, Littleover

DREAM ISLAND

Above my father's antique shop, I collapse into bed
I drift off to sleep and enter my world of dreams
I push at a rusty, splintered door and hear the hinges creak
Nervously, I step through the door and feel the sun beat down upon my face

I find myself on an island with sand as white as snow
Topaz waves, gently lapping at my bare feet
Turning, I see a smiley, young girl playing in the sun-kissed sand
My curiosity pulls me towards her

Taking my hand, she leads me around the island
Adventures like I've never known, fill my day
Swimming with playful dolphins in the tropical sea
Swinging through treetop canopies with cute, cuddly orangutans

As early evening arrives, we soar through the sky on majestic eagle backs
Then dig in the sand alongside leatherback turtles, anxious to lay their eggs
Her family arrive and we picnic together on the beach
Cheeky crabs scuttle over and steal our feast

The sun fades over the horizon as the sky turns sapphire-blue
Stars shine like diamonds as I peacefully fall asleep on the beach

The sound of my father's footsteps rouses me from my slumber
I can't wait to return to my dream island again tonight.

Grace Berry (11)
Littleover Community School, Littleover

ESCAPE

The treacherous feeling of fear is deep inside my heart,
It is like being captured in a wall of fiery flames.
Enclosed inside fears hurting my one and only soul,
Like ghosts haunting every moment of my life.
I am doomed...

Wailing, screaming, begging for help,
The feeling of torture and misery darken the days.
Shadows glooming everywhere,
What if I got hurt? What if I forgot something?
What if... what if...?
Worrying when certain events have not happened... yet.

Hoping and wishing,
Pleading and begging.
Closing my eyes and fighting the dark,
My heart and soul coming together as one.

Maybe there's a chance after all,
The ecstatic emotions, the feelings acting like one's shield.
Guarding my life and making it as bright as a day,
Glorious colours fill my head.

The hate goes away in a puff of smoke,
Bang!
I could feel my hands,
The furniture, the softness of a pillow.
It was like coming back to life again.

The chances were tough, the chances were thin,
But faith has come back.
Closing my eyes and fighting the dark,
The darkness has gone...
The sun comes again.

Zihan Qin (11)
Littleover Community School, Littleover

A TERRIBLE FEAR

I venture into the murky cave,
There are no sounds around me, save
My heart making sounds just like a drum,
My head is throbbing, fingers numb.

I'm terrified, with crawling skin,
I mutter last words as I tiptoe in,
I'm going to be enveloped in the dark,
But now the reality is stark.

They'll find me bleeding in the head,
What is it like to be dead?
A mystery unsolved, a case unclosed,
In eternal darkness, I will have dozed.

Now I hear scuttling all around,
Such a strange, unpleasant sound.
Now there is no diminishing light,
I know I will go without a fight.

I'm overcome with dread and despair,
I imagine a pitch-black monster's lair,
The scuttling sounds are coming near,
But it is not that which I fear.

The dark has been the horror of my life,
A cause of panic, a gnawing strife,

I'm longing for the cool, light air,
Suddenly, I'm out of the monster's lair.

The consequent joy and relief is great,
Everything is worth it, the fearful wait,
To return to the world I hold dear,
To escape from a terrible fear.

William Wright (11)
Littleover Community School, Littleover

SOLUTION TO POLLUTION

Pollution,
People say there's no solution:
So they just sit back,
Pretending they're just useless piles of sorry sacks.

Maybe they are,
As they smoke and release their fumes and tar.
Alongside
Their poisonous carbon dioxide.

But because of the damage we've caused,
There's no time to call each other frauds.
To those people who tried to warn you
Well, I think you owe them a few

And as the ozone layer breaks
I hope you grow more awake
To the fact that without each other,
We can say goodbye to one another

So all these charities you fight for:
#TIMESUP and Macmillan Cancer Support.
It won't matter, because as the sun burns down
In our useless charities, we will drown.

So go ahead and plant a tree,
And soon you'll be planting three.
Go get your bike out the shed,
Before you find that we're all dead.

So don't allow future generations
To ask if it was worth destroying our nations.
It's not too late to take a stand,
Because an eco-friendly land is what we demand.

Sumaira Azam (13)
Littleover Community School, Littleover

LIFE AT SCHOOL

Life at school gets my head in a whirl
Running here, running there makes my hair curl
First, it's English and I learn about Shakespeare
Then it's maths, and it's measure this sphere

Now I'm on break and I'm slapping Jake's head
It's easy to catch him, his brain's still in bed
Mustafa's chatting girls, but he's got it all wrong
Talking about study groups and how he's in set one

Next, it's geography, and we're yawning over rocks
Then it's technology, it's great making clocks
Finally, it's lunch, at last, I'm free
Only got to survive through the joy of RE

Paninis and crisps and I'm feeling great
Once I've played a game of tag, my clothes are in a state
Homework tonight, and it's science this time
Learning that making cows muscular, isn't a crime

I'm all in a flap and I gotta escape
The final lesson's over, it's time to make a break
Laughing all the way back home, and trying to entertain
Till tomorrow when the fun starts all over again.

Andrew Rodwell (13)
Littleover Community School, Littleover

CHANGE

Oh, the tower of Grenfell,
Just look at how it fell, after that, this news we had to tell.
Now we stand here, selling food and drink,
Especially for those people whose hearts really did sink.
Just look at those heartbroken people out somewhere,
If you look under their eye, you will see a tear trickling there.
With them, we should stand and share,
Deep in their heart, there will definitely be a tear.
Think about all the bad,
Which has made them thoroughly sad.
All those people who breathed their last,
Will not be forgotten very fast,
No matter who they are or what their cast.
The noise could be heard and not forgotten,
There were still some babies in their cots.
The fire was horrendous, it was also momentous.
Whilst everybody was insane,
The fire engines came.
This was just to take out the fire and
Fill everybody's desire.
Oh, the tower of Grenfell,
Just look at how it fell,
After that, everybody we had to tell.

Zoya Ali (11)
Littleover Community School, Littleover

THE FIRE

It is everywhere
Eating, consuming everything

Leaping, jumping, growing
I... am... petrified

It is petrified
You can see it in its face

Sitting there, frozen in the heat
Empty, useless extinguisher in its hands

All around me...
Everywhere...

Help!...
If there is any...

Ha, pathetic, little human,
It is nothing to me

I can crush all of them,
With a blow of my breath.

Argh, what is this?
A fire brigade

If there was one
Argh, shut up those hoses!

Not today, son
Go, go, go!

Move out, get this sorted
I want a perimeter check of the block

I can feel hands under me
Ahh, at last, relief...

"I don't think he is going to make it."
What, no! I must!

Pain, pain, pain
Darkness.

Henry Smith (12)
Littleover Community School, Littleover

ANGRY GUILT

The constant pain haunts you every day,
You're haunted by fear all the time.
It is always there, waiting for you,
Picking on your emotion.
The hatred builds up more and more,
Each time it comes, hatred is there.
Your feelings stop you lashing out,
But they will always build up.
Then it pushes you too far,
And then you break your guards.
An instant action has occurred,
You think it's right at the time,
But after it's happened, another emotion overcomes you.
Guilt.
For what it has done, you've done something worse.
The anger took control and changed you.
Now you've ruined it,
All you're left with is yourself to blame.
Now you have become it and it is the victim.
For all that it's worth,
You have changed.
There is no more innocence
It had gone for good
All that's left is what you have become
You should never tolerate bullying but never retaliate.

Tyler Hardwick (12)
Littleover Community School, Littleover

KNIFE CRIME

All around the world, people are dying,
All around the world, mothers are crying,
All around the world, people are lying,
And pretending they are high flying.

Knives, knives, more dangerous than beehives,
All they do is take innocent lives,
As innocent as five are not to survive,
As sad as it is, this is our lives.

When did the world become so cruel?
When did our children pick up these tools?
When did our children become such fools?
When did our children stop following the rules?

Let's stop it now, it's gone too far,
It's left us all with a scar,
We've put so many behind bars,
Never to see another star.

So, stop children!
Put it away,
Enough innocence has gone away
So, stop this war
Let's do it no more
Let's make this place
A safer space!

Zaibaa Tair (12)
Littleover Community School, Littleover

PRISON

I somehow managed to escape the prison
they all call it school
I found myself in the woods
this is where I normally go
to escape the leashes of life
I climb trees to let out my emotions
I wish I could let go and fall an endless fall
But I can't
so I climb back down
I lie on the cold, dead leaves
I wonder if this is how it feels to be dead
Suddenly, I feel like something is watching me
I look. I see two red eyes that seem to be full of blood
I can't escape the creatures glare
I think, *should I let it get me?*
No
I run as fast as a bullet entering an enemy's flesh
then I climb up the tree
I look down
I can't see it anymore
I look up
and there it is
the jaws of death staring right at me
I know there is no escape

Then I suddenly find myself at school
and everyone looking at me
and the teacher wanting an answer from me.

Shabbir Ali Raja (13)
Littleover Community School, Littleover

FOR THIS IS HALLOWEEN

It's glowing in the dark,
But with an eerie spark,
This spine-chilling night,
Is down to give you a fright,
This night will make you scream,
For this is Halloween.

This is a nightmare, not a dream,
Vampires are drinking from a bloodstream,
Evil spirits and witches are near,
But don't you try and run my dear,
This night will make you scream,
For this is Halloween.

Streets filled with ominous clowns,
Turning little children's smiles to frowns,
The light of pumpkins guiding you on your street,
Make sure you be careful of who you meet,
This night will make you scream,
For this Halloween.

You've got to hurry, be on your way,
The parents will take the sweets away,
Fireworks will be shooting up high,

You'll see them blasting through the sky,
This night will make you scream,
For this is Halloween.

Harleen Dhamrait (12)
Littleover Community School, Littleover

THE ADVENTURE INTO THE UNKNOWN!

Today will be an adventure.
Today will be a discovery,
I am brave,
I can let all my fears go,
I am not afraid to walk on thin ice.

Today I will close the door to the past.
Today I will open a door to the future,
Life is unknown,
Life is strange,
I am not afraid of the dark,
I am brave,
I am ready,
I am not afraid of the dark.

A wall stood in front of me,
A blanket of snow pillowed my feet,
I was careful of the journey I took,
As footprints will show,
And people will know,
The future is unknown,
The future is a mystery
The adventure starts today.

Behind the wall will be a mystery,
Behind the wall will be untold,
One more step,
Until life will change,
One more step,
Until I will change,
The future will be untold,
The future is a mystery,
The adventure starts today.

Sophie Buxton (12)
Littleover Community School, Littleover

THE SOLE SURVIVOR

I walk along the broken roads
I see what society once was
I recollect the thoughts of my life
And those who I've lost

I walk along the broken roads
I see the shells of what once were homes
I remember my dreams of the future
And how shattered they are

I walk along the broken roads
I see the abominations which lurk in the shadows
I remember my daughter
And how I lost her to them

I walk along the broken roads
I see our desperate attempts to save ourselves
I remember thinking we would be okay
And I was ever so wrong

I walk along the broken roads
I see those who have passed on
I remember their faces
And now they're just skulls

I walk along the broken roads
I see what society once was

I recollect thoughts of my life
And those who I've lost.

Thomas Fowler (13)
Littleover Community School, Littleover

AUDITION LINEUP

Around sixty dancers shaking with fright
all dressed up in leotards and tights

We all sit down and stretch out our muscles
While mums and dads hustle and bustle

We pin on our numbers, getting pricked a little
as we get called in, we whisper and giggle

We stand in a line with our feet in the first position
as the teacher starts to talk, all the dancers listen

We quickly learn the steps of the dance
around the room, we leap and prance

Most of the dancers have what it takes
If we walk together, there's no room for mistakes

As we finish, we curtsey and bow
We all hope we have got in somehow

All that's left is a waiting game
Will the cast list contain my name?

I get the email and read it through
I got in, there's no need to feel blue.

Lizzie Bellamy (12)
Littleover Community School, Littleover

GRENFELL TOWER

Grenfell, oh Grenfell, how you fell.
Millions of people we had to tell.
Many people died but some still survived.
We all pray until this very day.
All our hearts were broken in every way.
Those who were living are now dead.
Those who were breathing are from the living Earth fled.
We all knew that the news would spread.
We could see a man wipe a tear from his eye,
but for those who lost their loved ones, had to say goodbye.
Those who are now in ashes lay beneath the ground.
Those who were affected screamed out loud.
Artists came together to sing a song for Grenfell,
Bridge Over Troubled Water will be a song which will never be forgotten.
It's been more than a year and the tower is still standing
A few years will come and the tower will be longstanding
Rest In Peace to the people who were affected.

Saba Ashraf (11)
Littleover Community School, Littleover

I'M AN EVACUEE

I am now an evacuee
Shall I wonder what the world has in store for me?
I leave my family
I guess this is who I am meant to be
I am on my way to the train
Then it starts to rain
I glance out of the window
There are a lot of kids in here
They all have the same fear
We finally arrive at our destination
And we get off the station
I wonder if someone will pick me
Whose new child will I be?
I wonder and wonder
And then it starts to thunder
Someone comes and looks at me
Examining my body
She goes and talks to the person who took the children
I try and hear but there are millions
The lady comes back
And she says, "Grab your sack."
I am so relieved
I'm finally leaving
I have a new family

I am now so happy!

Imaan Ali (11)
Littleover Community School, Littleover

CALL OF THE HAUNTED

I heard the sound...
A hurricane of destruction swept over the landscape.
What was once a jewel of the natural world,
was now a harbour of destruction.
The first machine of decimation began with a deafening roar,
I heard it sever the trunk of my cousin as if it was enjoying it.
Powerfully, the ballistic bulldozer roared to life,
It was heading for me...
Without even stopping to notice my fellow family,
it trampled on, sweeping through my kin.
Sorrowfully, a tear of pain and anguish trickled down
my withered bark.
Then it hit me...
I could feel the blades pierce my base
and puncture my oozy sap,
I could feel the agony in my trunk as I fell to my doom.
Everything after that was red.
The flame engulfed me. The last leaf burnt to a crisp.

Jack Williams (11)
Littleover Community School, Littleover

CHANGE

Throw away hatred; spread only love,
Turn a vulture into a peaceful dove.
Open the gates of the big prison,
We all know there is a reason.

There is a feeling,
but there is no meaning.
The playmates who really care,
Are very rare.

A simple thought,
In which my mind is caught.
Can always light hope in us,
As it has the chance to adjust.

There may be a tear,
Which brings no fear.
It could be for a mild change,
Which may be a bit strange.

To reflect on the year,
Would create a good cheer.
The journey starts with a step,
It's definitely a good prep.

Having to move fast,
It needs to be left in the past.

A bit of change every now and again,
Can save us from facing a lot of pain.

Christy Jince (12)
Littleover Community School, Littleover

CHANGE

Changes can be seen in the leaves on the trees,
As the seasons go by with a breeze
Hot weather, cold weather,
wet and dry whatever the weather
look to the sky.
Spring high, it's time to fly,
keep warm and nice and dry.
The birds have vanished,
the snow has appeared, stick a hat on to cover those ears.
Splish, splosh, the rain is here, get a brolly it will be needed today.
Spring is in the air, winter is in the past
new growth everywhere, growing really fast
Animals come out finally, after all that,
soon, mothers are having offspring as the new ones arrive.
Shining bright in the sky, a beam of light appears
everyone is cheering because it is finally the holidays
Planes going left and right, taking people for a holiday delight.

Katie Louise Birks (11)
Littleover Community School, Littleover

WELCOME TO THE FUTURE

Let me tell you a rhyme,
About another time,
Magical powers can become true,
With the colour of technology, which is blue,
Flying cars rapidly zooming around,
Then safely landing flat on the ground.

Security is so very advanced,
Robbers and burglars have no chance,
Hear the silent sound of trains going at the speed of light,
As you go past a kid with his never-ending kite.
Drones and robots, can they really take over?

Travelling to Mars, that's nothing,
Travelling to another galaxy, well, that's something,
Now let's talk about virtual reality, yeah, the real deal,
It's very fake but also extremely real!
Now that you know it all,
Maybe you would like to go to the future where poetry really escapes...

Safiyah Khan (11)
Littleover Community School, Littleover

THE NEXT VICTIM

I carefully selected my next victim,
The weak, the less able,
I planned it out,
As if they were my prey.

I pounced, ready,
The mouse was in the trap,
All guns loaded,
Fire!

I took her back,
Dragged her to the house of doom,
She tried to fight back,
Screaming, shouting.

I strangled her,
Blood showered the floor,
The knife in and out,
I couldn't control it.

She fell to the floor,
As blood surrounded her,
Why did I just do that?
How could I just do that?

The knife found its way into my hand,
Pointing towards me,

I took one last breath
I collapsed onto the stone, bitter floor.

Sienna Sagoo (12)
Littleover Community School, Littleover

CHANGE

The fields are rich with daffodils,
A coat of clover coats the hills.
When it is time for spring,
The birds always seem to sing.

The Earth is warm, the sun's ablaze
It is a time of carefree days;
When the days are very long,
Nothing ever seems to go wrong.

The leaves are red, yellow and brown,
A shower sprinkles softly down;
The air is fragrant, crisp and cool,
And once again, I'm stuck at school.

The birds are gone, the world is white,
The winds are wild, they chill and bite.
Whenever I want to play around,
There is snow piling up on the frozen ground.

Spring, summer, autumn, snow,
This is how each year must go.

Khaira Ahmed (11)
Littleover Community School, Littleover

THE MAGIC MESS

My cauldron bubbled,
And my potions fizzed,
It banged and boomed,
And popped and whizzed.

My toads started to sing,
My birds started to crow,
Just how long it would last,
I really didn't know.

Hinkypunks and pigglypuffs,
Were getting out of hand,
Running riot around my feet,
Making it hard to stand.

Magic wands were zapping,
And pixie's wings were flapping,
And what's that thing where Pumpkin's sat?
My special magic hat?

Until...

Yes!
everything back as normal,
The way it had started out,
Books on the shelves and potions away,
Just the way I like it!

Bronwyn Wigley (13)
Littleover Community School, Littleover

THE SEA

Blue and wavy, rolling around,
Takes a while to touch the ground.
Boats snaking across your vast form,
Fish awaken from their personal dorm.

Crabs furrowing through your sand,
The sea, oh, what a beautiful land.
Your treasure, the clam with the pearl,
Your whirlpools, majestic, give us a twirl.

Dolphins jumping up and down,
I wonder about the divers, how they don't drown.
The shark, the king of the sea,
When it comes near, need the smaller fish flee?

Whales, the biggest of them all,
Across your chassis, they quietly call.
"We love you, Sea, wide and tall,
You are the greatest of all!"

Jacob Curd (11)
Littleover Community School, Littleover

THE FUTURE BEYOND/BEYOND DESTINY

Destiny and faith say it all,
Each step you take is planned,
God knows what your next move is,
No need to take the matter into your hands.

All around you,
Is nature, life, aliveness,
Don't let it go to waste,
Take control of your tiredness.

You get second chances,
For a reason,
Only if you're lucky enough,
Will you get the achievement.

Never give up,
Try, try, harder and better,
One day you'll see,
Your success and your treasure.

Keep and hold within you,
The power you behold,
And then you'll realise,
Your future beyond...

Mariya Hussain (13)
Littleover Community School, Littleover

DIVERSITY

Stop!
You're not buying those cookies,
Due to the specific intention, you will put on weight,
Who would like obese people in this world?
I do!
Everyone is different,
Some people were and will be different, but it's perfectly fine,
It is the thing which forms us to be unique,
Which fascinated me,
Seven point five billion people in this world,
No two alike,
Everyone is different,
We like it like this!
Now go get those cookies,
Be who you would like to be,
You're unique in your own sense of form.
Fly free like wild birds.

Haider Ali Irfan (13)
Littleover Community School, Littleover

RHYMING COUPLETS

Cars sounding loud
poisonous smoke forming clouds
people just don't care
comfortably polluting the air
we need to save our plants
animals, insects and even little ants
we need to unite to stop this pollution
otherwise, we will live in delusion
no plants, no trees
melting ice caps and rising seas
destruction, suffering and unimaginable pain
so much loss and very little gain
If we let our plants die
our life will just be a lie
let us stand together and unite
for a common goal, we must *fight*.

Huzayfah Shaid (13)
Littleover Community School, Littleover

CHANGE - WHAT YOU CAN DO!

When you see litter in the streets
And the air smells of pollution
When you feel like it's all piling up
Remember there is a solution

There's something each of us can do
To keep the rivers clean
To keep fresh the air we breathe
And keep the forests green

Help clean a beach
Or recycle bottles and cans
Learn about the problems we face
And help others understand

It doesn't have to be a lot
If we each just do our share
So take time on Earth Day
To show Earth you care.

Alisha Mahmood (13)
Littleover Community School, Littleover

AN ODE TO AUTUMN

The leaves drop gently from the trees,
Falling slowly to the ground.
Swaying, dancing in the breeze,
Laying a carpet all around.
As the temperature turns cold,
The autumn leaves come again.
The red and gold leaves are bold,
The sun goes away and here comes the rain.
Bonfire night comes with a boom,
Children in bed, all tucked up and cosy.
On clear nights, they look at the moon,
Cheeks from the wind all blushed up and rosy.
Now it's time for Christmas Eve,
To see what tricks Santa has up his sleeve.

Katie House (11)
Littleover Community School, Littleover

TRUTH OR DARE?

Into the darkness, I reach out a hand,
Where shadows play and light is banned.
My breaths decline and I gasp for air,
This has become a deadly game of truth or dare.
Do I dare to escape from this place?
Run away from memories of your face?
Do I speak the truth of how I feel?
How the love still there is very much real.
My heart pulses and beats ever so slow,
Of the pain and suffering, you will never get to know.
My body becomes weary and falls so weak,
Then I disappear into dreams of despair, for the meek.

Jazmine Hafez (12)
Littleover Community School, Littleover

CREATURES

The creatures I fear are fleshy and pale,
Have rectangular teeth and don't have a tail.
Some are large, some are lean,
And every single one of them is very, very mean.
When they see you they are never quiet,
And when you get close they start a riot.
They keep a furry mouse on their head,
They go into a box which is where they shed.
And when you spot a small one on its own,
It will let out a roar or a very loud groan.
Even though they are what I fear,
They never get close, don't even come near.

Sonny Rooney (12)
Littleover Community School, Littleover

DROWNING IN PLASTIC

It seems like everyone has forgotten,
the old and the young,
just how vulnerable the Earth may be
Coral, seals and other life in the sea,
know how difficult life can be.

Plastic in the ocean, out of reach
sometimes it ends up on a beach.
This is where it becomes drastic,
animals are unknowingly eating plastic.

We need to take a minute and think,
before buying another water bottle to drink
All we can do now is hope
and figure out a way to cope.

Shifa Aziz (12)
Littleover Community School, Littleover

CHANGE

This is what I have to say,
that all of you should know,
our history is fading away,
but I don't want to go.

I wish I could turn back time,
before the future came,
before someone committed a crime,
or people starting to invent fame.

From people wearing bonnets,
to skin-tight ripped jeans,
and here I am, writing a sonnet,
not listening to music from 2018.

All I know is the world is rearranging.
How can we stop it from changing?

Naila Mustafa (12)
Littleover Community School, Littleover

THE GAME THAT LASTED

We buy them
We play them
Then we leave
And forget about them
Then we click repeat
Without thinking
Without looking
Just doing
It's like we have to
But sometimes
On that special occasion
When we don't click repeat
But we play and we play
And we carry on playing
Until the end of our days
That special occasion
For me, and for everyone
is *life*
It lasted
Until the end of our days.

Oliver Young (12)
Littleover Community School, Littleover

A VOICE

Imagine a world where you didn't have a voice.
Going with everything,
without a choice.

Where you couldn't decide,
What you had for tea.
Where you couldn't scream,
Getting stung by a bee.

Some people don't decide,
What happens to their lives.
Their country, people,
They even have their rooms painted purple.

A voice in life is a great thing.
Speak out!

Torsten Ellis (13)
Littleover Community School, Littleover

STOP ANIMAL ABUSE!

Tied to a post, all dirty and cold
The animal is starting to become old

He wheezes and cries
He pulls at his ties

The paws are sore
As he waits at the door

His cries are lonely and sad
How do you not feel bad?

Poor old boy, he is alone
As you sit there upon your throne

You are evil, so stop now! I'm serious
Don't be so delirious.

Jessica Louise Angel Bird (12)
Littleover Community School, Littleover

POEM ON CHANGE

Change is inevitable,
Change will always happen.
The Earth is changing,
We are changing the Earth.
We are ruining what was made,
by past generations.
We are ruining the seas,
putting plastic in it as if the sea was a junkyard.

We are changing, we have been since the Earth began,
you can't deny that.
But this time, *change*, is what might just ruin us all.

Claudia Holmes (12)
Littleover Community School, Littleover

JUNGLE ADVENTURES

Terrestrial plants
The air is humid and damp
Vines cling to tall trees

An abyss-blue stream
Winding through dense undergrowth
Lush foliage swaying

The lions are growling
Paws crunching leaves noisily
Crunch, crackle, crunch, crackle, crunch!

Their eyes, a black void
But their mane full of colour
Majestic and bold.

Abigail Maia Morgan (11)
Littleover Community School, Littleover

AUTUMN IS HERE

Leaves are falling
Yellow and brown
Autumn is here
It's all around

Reds are swirling
Yellow is flying
Green is staying
The gold is glistening

Swirling, swishing
Sliding down
Autumn is here
It's all around

I stomp in the mud
Swash in the puddles
Crunch go the leaves
Autumn is here.

Megan Hurn (12)
Littleover Community School, Littleover

SEASONS

Haiku poetry

First flower of spring,
fruit grows, animals are born,
warm, fresh scented air.

Summer is scorching,
relaxing on the hot sand,
enjoying ice cream.

Red, yellow and brown,
the leaves dance in the cool breeze,
winter will come soon.

The snow is falling,
snowball fights, building snowmen,
fires are lit all round.

Nia Carey Swain (11)
Littleover Community School, Littleover

HIEROGLYPHS, ART, PLANES AND COMPUTERS

Haiku poetry

Hieroglyphs on walls,
Large tombs built for great pharoahs,
Pyramids stood tall.

Art gained more detail,
Buildings had grander structures,
Discoveries made.

Planes started to fly,
Telephones came to be used,
Cars started to drive.

Computers are owned,
Helicopters fly up high,
Touchscreens are now used.

Jenny Cameron (12)
Littleover Community School, Littleover

ON A MOUNTAIN

On a mountain,
Not too far away,
A girl is living,
Living wild,
Living cold,
Living with no constraints.
But wishing for family,
Wishing for comfort,
Wishing for faith.
But knowing nothing,
Knowing no joy,
Knowing only pain.
Not too far away,
On a mountain.

Evie Kininmonth (12)
Littleover Community School, Littleover

CHANGES ALL AROUND US!

Things are growing every moment
All night and day
Things are changing all around us -
In a hundred different ways
Can't you see the seasons changing?
Winter is turning into spring
Can't you hear the birds announce it?
Listen to them sing!

Tanisha Latif (11)
Littleover Community School, Littleover

FELINE FANTASY

What do you think of me?
As I pounce on your lap, which is as rough as a dreary old rock,
You think I care about you.
My teeth tear through your flesh.
The iron-y taste of your blood is a potion of strength.
At this, I liven into a fearsome lion whilst you scream in agony, yelling.

I'm the king, here!
I journey off to my desired den,
My branch high up in the air.
No one can defeat me, not even the best of men.
In a fight (with me) there is no such thing as fair.
I am a mighty warrior!

You hunger to know my weakness?
But, I am as black as the night.
The sound of my treats is a ringing bell - calling for my presence.

Beware!
For, I'm always aware.
You'll stroke me.
I'll turn and say, "You dare!"
I'm not fair.

But then you pick me up!
I'm defenceless.
I scramble my legs,
Unable to move.
Panic builds and courses through me.
I'm locked away to go to sleep,
So here I lie.

Alasdair Rowan (12)
Lutterworth High School, Lutterworth

DIVERGENT

Who are we truly, deep down inside?
Are we:
Dauntless - brave,
Erudite - intelligent,
Abnegation - selfless (stiffs),
Candour - honest?

Who truly knows,
Do we know?
Do our parents know?
Does anyone know?
Who are we?

Who are we truly, deep down inside?
Are we:
Dauntless - brave,
Erudite - intelligent,
Abnegation - selfless (stiffs),
Candour - honest.

Or are we divergent...?

Grace Ann Harrison (12)
Lutterworth High School, Lutterworth

TRICK OR TREATING

Trick or treating is the thing I love more than my aunts washing tub.
When I knock on the door to say trick or treat, my heart skips a beat
They open the door and say hi, but then I begin to cry
They pat me on my shoulder but unfortunately, they push me over!
They say, "Sorry about that."
Me on the floor saying, "I like your welcome mat."
Their mask is very scary, he says, "Don't worry, my name is Jerry."
As I am picking my sweets off the floor, I hear a roar from next door.
So I investigate over there to find a witch in her lair.
I scream for my life but it is only Jerry's wife.
I will have to wait a year to have another fright,
thank goodness it only happens once on Halloween night!

Myles Rowley
Quinton House School, Northampton

DEAR TIME TRAVELLING MACHINE...

Dear time travelling machine,
I can never see you, but you are always there,
You are invisible, you must be somewhere,

I don't know what, or who you are,
Although I know you can't be far,

Sometimes I think I'm mad,
I don't know, maybe it's really bad,

I must be dreaming, I must,
I can't tell, I don't know who to trust,

Every night as I go to bed,
A thousand thoughts go through my head,

I love this mystery time machine,
It shows me things no one gets to see,

What or who could you be?
I can't think, it's like catching a flea,

You seem to take me when I'm thinking,
Hmm, what do I do when I'm thinking?

I sit in silence and eat,
But what is it that I eat?

I'm nearly there, I've nearly solved it,
I think I know it, I now can admit,

My happiness is in the fridge,
Not anywhere grand, not over a bridge,

Dear time travelling machine,
I eat you when I'm thinking,
You carry me to happiness,

Dear time travelling machine,
You are a pineapple.

Tessa Smith (12)
Sir Thomas Boughey Academy, Halmerend

DEPRESSION

I'm afraid of the world.
Not things in it, the people in it.
Why did it have to be me? Why not them?
Depression isn't something we can get rid of,
or ignore
People don't choose if they have it,
it chooses them
It's not fair.

Depression is a disease that affects every aspect of my life.
It's not like I don't want to be happy,
it's despite how hard I try,
Yet I can't bring myself to be happy.

I feel embarrassed, ashamed and then I think to myself,
Why did I have to be this way?
I have a great family, amazing family.
Yet I close my eyes and it's still there.

Yet all I ever seem to see is sadness and grey,
It's like there's this thing on me, making it hard to move
I just want to get away from my body and go somewhere else
Living has been this constant nightmare and fear
of everything, everybody and myself.

Hannah Gallimore (11)
Sir Thomas Boughey Academy, Halmerend

SAFETY

Safety, a refuge, in trouble or afraid
for those in need of help or those in need of aid
but what is safety other than another place to contemplate?
What is safety but another place to hide, or write a complaint?
Safety is a prison when you think of safety, you think of home
You don't think of going out and exploring abroad in Rome
So is safety really what you want instead of being free?
Or is it just a setback to your potential and key
Do not hate safety, your friend, your pillow to fall upon
But don't overuse it as it's a pair of hands holding you down
The spot where you have stood for so long, but didn't notice
Until today, so I say, break from your chains, go to China or Detroit
Just don't stay there forever, the outside world isn't as bad as it seems
So enjoy your safety, cherish it
I'm not going to stop you, just see, behind the scenes.

Oliver Birch (13)
Sir Thomas Boughey Academy, Halmerend

THE HOUSE ON THE HILL

The house on the hill stands alone and dark,
But when the clock strikes twelve, the adventure will spark.
The once dark windows flicker a flame,
Is the house empty or is it a game?

The sounds of a piano can be heard,
Tinkling keys, how absurd
I'm scared but drawn,
As I tiptoe across the muddy lawn.

Leaving my footprints behind,
Something suddenly comes to mind.
Next to my prints are another set,
Leading right up to the bottom step.

The door is ajar,
"Come join us," a voice calls from afar.
I follow the voice into the house,
All the noise stops and it falls as quiet as a mouse.

As I pause to decide my fate,
The door slams behind me and it's too late...

Ellie-May Worrall (12)
Sir Thomas Boughey Academy, Halmerend

THE MATCH

It's finally here, it's finally the day -
Match day's here and I'm on my way
Football's back and summer's over
as the pitch of green is being graced again
The walk to the stadium is a magical stroll
But when you're on the pitch
The fairy tale ends
The away fans come in small batches
but pack a punch
But not the ones who have been drinking since lunch
The net ripples as the crowd goes wild
My heart thumps as the crowd O'leys!
As I know the journey home
will be fun and positive
The whistle is blown and the crowd erupts
As the match is over and we all head home
as I wonder what will happen
on my next adventure.

Harry Hulse (12)
Sir Thomas Boughey Academy, Halmerend

MY ODE TO THE OAK TREE

Ancient oak tree
You're as old as fate
and as old as knowledge
Yet when you die, all is lost
but when you live, all is known
I love your possibilities
they are endless
I love to think of all you have seen
all the people who have sat under your leaves
How many animals have lived in your branches?
How many acorns have fallen from your ancient arms?
Your ancient branches that see no lies
Yet see no truth
You last as long as time itself
You shall not rot, you shall not wither
But you shall stand tall in the meadow
for many years to come
your acorns shall fall and grow
into many more generations of
the mighty, ancient oak.

Damian Wilson (12)
Sir Thomas Boughey Academy, Halmerend

TICK-TOCK

Tick-tock, the time travelling robot,
That's me.
I've been from place to place,
for what seems like forever now.
I have witnessed the Earth from birth to death,
Every animals' first to last breath.

Woven like a thread,
Into the past

Now it is time I go into the opposite direction
To the next day
Next week
Next year
And beyond
To see what has never been seen
To read books that have not yet been written

I may only be a robot,
Yet, I have dreams.
I have places to go, places to see.

Three...
Two...
One...

Time to go down the rabbit hole.

Shi Alisha Koroma (13)
Sir Thomas Boughey Academy, Halmerend

DECADES FROM NOW

Towers and buildings as tall as the sky,
Huge crowds of people, strangers passing by,
Clean walls and rows of windows gleaming and bright,
Pearly white structures, reach an intimidating height.

Trains and cars whizzing around, as fast as light,
The metallic cities illuminated at night,
Silhouettes stand out in the dark, as sharp as knives,
Always that just get darker, from light they are deprived.

Technology so advanced, it's always right,
Magical interactive screens, made of light
Books with pages that phase through your hand
Has humanity come too far? they ask. Yes.
And all for a prize made of sand.

Isobel Mary Connolly (12)
Sir Thomas Boughey Academy, Halmerend

THE ANGEL TRAPPED IN HELL

I'm trapped inside a dungeon,
Sealed behind a door.
I used to fly in the sunsets,
But never any more.

Sacred dreams are hidden,
In the land, where all is forbidden.
Everything locked away in here dies,
Then end up where the cursed key lies.

Find it, bind it, break the curse.
You'll find everything in reverse.

Begin to believe,
You'll start to retrieve.
Everything to lead the way,
Will come to you within a day.

These dirty walls,
Hide the calls,
of anyone who tries to save me.

Maddison Rose Pemberton (11)
Sir Thomas Boughey Academy, Halmerend

AN ODE TO SPACE

As I look into the eyes of space
I see the breathtaking stars glisten and twinkle
In the neverending darkness

A nebula explosion fills space with vibrant colours
those colours can be seen light years away

I think of all the other mysterious things
we don't see or know about that still lurk in space

As a supernova outshines galaxies and radiates energy
I wonder what life would be like without space
Would we even exist?

But for now, I don't need to worry
because space is here and always will be here.

Nakisha Lei Evans (12)
Sir Thomas Boughey Academy, Halmerend

PIRATE'S LIFE

We sail the seven seas at dusk
Over time our boats will rust
We sail to find what we seek
Under our feet, the floorboards creak

The old man is crazy, we call him Old Knocker
Soon, he'll find his way to Davy Jones' Locker

People say it's where you find the treasure
to a pirate's ears, it sounds like a pleasure

We all chug a pint of beer
and chant my name of Blackbeard
Most people will feel fear
But there's one pirate that makes fear afraid of him
By the name of Captain Jack Sparrow.

Leighton Pugh (13)
Sir Thomas Boughey Academy, Halmerend

CHRISTMAS

I went to the North Pole,
I jumped down a hole,
It was Santa's workshop,
I hit the bottom, *plop!*
I walked around,
Santa's inbound,
Oh no, he saw me,
I really needed to flee,
"Can I have your house key?"
he said.
His voice resonating in my head,
He was taking me home,
I sat on his knee bone,
On the sleigh, we flew away,
He took me to my room,
The sleigh went, *boom!*
on the roof,
I lost my tooth,
I went to sleep,
After I had counted sheep.

Oscar James Campbell (12)
Sir Thomas Boughey Academy, Halmerend

JUST BECAUSE

Just because I don't look like you,
Why do you hurt me too?

I don't want to come to school
Because you make my life so cruel
Day in, day out,
You keep chasing me about
It's a never-ending circle of life,
You always seem to carry strife

I'm no grass,
I'm no stitch,
But this is really giving me an internal itch
Dare I shout,
Dare I speak,
For the help I must seek?
I shall not stand for it any longer,
I promise I will become stronger!

Gracie Rondel (13)
Sir Thomas Boughey Academy, Halmerend

THE UNICORN

I saw a unicorn
Chewing on the lawn
Then I finished my tea
Then I saw a bee
Buzzing all alone
So then I went on my phone
Then I saw the horn on the unicorn
Glowing in the air
Then I ate a pear
Then I went into the pool
Then after ten minutes, I got a tool
and I broke the wall
So now I'm going to fall
Aargh!
Waah!
Now I'm going to send
this to you, my friend.
The end!

Christopher Babb (11)
Sir Thomas Boughey Academy, Halmerend

THE HOSPITAL VISIT

Haiku poetry

It makes you afraid,
It makes you panic-stricken,
It makes you upset.

Hospital visit,
Makes me tearful and so sad,
Seeing all the beds.

My grandpa lying,
There in his comfortable bed,
Kisses on the cheek.

Treatment is working,
Grandpa is up on his feet,
Is this all a dream?

Making me happy,
Thought of him being okay,
Grandpa coming home.

Jessica Clay (11)
Sir Thomas Boughey Academy, Halmerend

BOOKS

Haiku poetry

I like reading books,
They're very interesting,
Fiction, non-fiction,

Reading lots of books,
Makes me feel very relaxed,
They are comforting,

Harry Potter books,
I lose myself inside them,
I like Twilight too,

Enid Blyton books,
They are really good to read,
I enjoy reading,

Books.

Laila Olivia Yates (11)
Sir Thomas Boughey Academy, Halmerend

THE XBOX

When I get home
I am always on my Xbox
I am mostly playing games
instead of watching YouTube
Lots of players trying to win
if they don't,they hit themselves with a pin

Some even take a dumb test
Most of them don't even say yes
Millions of players are now getting frustrated
Some of them are just appreciated.

Comfort Sellers (11)
Sir Thomas Boughey Academy, Halmerend

THE BEACH

As I run across the golden sand
All I think about is the land
The smell of chips in my nose
I wonder what my family chose

As I splash around in the sea
Oh no, I dropped my key!
As I'm playing
My mum's bathing

My brothers playing
My nan's in a meeting
I love chips
I now have salty lips.

Kacey Williams (11)
Sir Thomas Boughey Academy, Halmerend

MY LOVE OF DRIVING

The feeling of excitement when you
step into the car

The nerves about what's ahead
Will I win or lose?

How many cars will I overtake?
One, two, three or more?

Will I win for the team
or will I have to be pushed over the line?

I was in-between
But everyone goes home with a smile.

James Nicholas Endall (13)
Sir Thomas Boughey Academy, Halmerend

MY DOG

My dog is named Stanley
He is in my family
Whenever he goes for a run
He always finds it so much fun
He has some dog friends who are boys
And he also has a lot of toys
He also loves to sleep, but when he wants a great big treat
He loves to do a massive leap
My dog Stanley is a big part of my family.

Gabriella Jayne Healey (13)
Sir Thomas Boughey Academy, Halmerend

RAINFOREST JOURNEY

Haiku poetry

Raining rainforest
Hearing noisy animals
This is the jungle

High canopy trees
Walking on sludgy, wet grass
I am getting drenched

Predators hiding
I need to keep an eye out
I am in danger

The calming noises
You can fall asleep with ease
I am at peace now.

Sophie Grace Jervis (11)
Sir Thomas Boughey Academy, Halmerend

GOODBYE...

You like
You cry
You say goodbye

You lie
You're saying you're okay
but sigh
Saying it's just your eyes watering
but you die
inside

You fake smile
but it starts to turn vile
Too young, too innocent
Just my time to say
goodbye.

Olivia Windsor (13)
Sir Thomas Boughey Academy, Halmerend

HALLOWEEN SCARES

On one dark, gloomy day,
We all went to play,
To share a fright,
In the middle of the night.
Children playing outside their homes,
OMG, I saw some bones.
Vampires biting,
And zombies frightening,
See you tomorrow,
Where you will find your dead sorrow.

Alissa-Rose Graham (11)
Sir Thomas Boughey Academy, Halmerend

THE FUTURE

Let's think about what's to come
About what we could become,
Maybe a policeman, doctor or a dentist,
Or even an apprentice,
Maybe there will be flying cars,
I could even be behind bars,
I hope that's not the truth,
And I'll be under my own roof.

Kian Windsor Finney (13)
Sir Thomas Boughey Academy, Halmerend

MYSTERY MOUNTAIN

Haiku poetry

Mountains soaring high
Above the clouds and the birds
What a sight to see

Snowy peaks up high
Swirling mist, wonderful sight
Hidden paths to find

Winding here and there
Treasures hidden everywhere
What will we find there?

Crystal Knott (11)
Sir Thomas Boughey Academy, Halmerend

ADVENTURE

Everybody needs an adventure
from the biggest to the smallest ones
The feeling of freedom
of having no limits
The new experiences
Having no rules to obey
Living as wild as can be
The wind blowing your hair.

Tia Lily Pemberton (12)
Sir Thomas Boughey Academy, Halmerend

HOLIDAYS

Holidays are fun
Because instead of going on my PS4
I spend time with my mum
When I spend time with my family
It always manages to make me happy
Even though I moan at my brother
We will always love each other.

Joshua Luke Knott (12)
Sir Thomas Boughey Academy, Halmerend

CATS

As fluffy as can be,
When you cuddle me in the cold,
If you dig your claws into me,
Your biggest secret will be told,
That you are not a fighter jet,
But actually, my adorable pet.

Daisy Westwood (12)
Sir Thomas Boughey Academy, Halmerend

DANCE

Disco, tap, contemporary
Dancing, dancing side to side
Acro, stage, modern
Moving side to side
Flick, kick, spin, turn around,
Yay!
Up, down, round and round.

Millie Reay (12)
Sir Thomas Boughey Academy, Halmerend

CHEESECAKE IS GREAT

Cheesecake is the king of cake
It is so great
It is the greatest thing to be -
invented in history
Why it was invented, I think -
continues to be a mystery.

Calum David Wintle (13)
Sir Thomas Boughey Academy, Halmerend

ABDUCTED?

A boy and his friend were out on a walk,
When a sudden, loud noise interrupted their talk,
A spaceship hovered above his head,
What will happen next? he thought, with dread,
Up and up and up he rose,
From the tip of his ears to the end of his toes.

He could see four aliens covered in drool,
This was worse than being at school,
He thought he was toast,
Or even a Sunday roast,
He thought he'd never go back,
Then everything went black.

They asked lots of questions because he was clever,
Did he answer them? No, not ever,
It seemed like he'd been up there forever, all alone,
He missed his family, he missed his home,
Inside his head, he did a scream,
Then he woke up in bed, it had all been a dream.

Matthew Kimberlin (11)
The William Allitt School, Newhall

DOOMSDAY!

The Armageddon
The final battle,
The showdown between good and evil.

Smelling the flavourless smoke
As we wake up limbless,
In the air, a tasteless breeze
As I look to find the moon fearless.

No sun, no rain
No nothing to see,
Rising up to the boneless bodies
... The catastrophe!

Demolished buildings
Dust devouring the cities,
Shocked and anxious emotions
Rubble and grit plastering families!

The lives of innocents
Being taken away,
Humongous, raging crowds
Shouts and screams coming my way...

Run away! Get away!
They're crying to the...

Armageddon
Final battle,

The showdown has finished
Between evil and me!

Aimee Grace Patrick (14)
The William Allitt School, Newhall

NIGHTMARES

Early morning, 7 o'clock,
I rose out of bed,
ready to put on my clothes for the day ahead,

As I stepped down the stairs,
I looked in front of me,
to see the world's biggest adventure,
waiting for me.

As I walked out the door,
it was a new world,
full of mystery,
out into the woodlands,
I could hear, what sounded like
a troubled deer.

So I went over to see,
to discover it was a deer,
but he wasn't in a hurry;
he said to me,
"Eat these magical jelly beans,
and you will see,
that one of your nightmares will be a forgotten mystery."
So I got home and went to bed,
and there wasn't a single nightmare in my head.

Chloe Morgan Bradbury (11)
The William Allitt School, Newhall

A RAINBOW OF EMOTIONS

Blue is for when I'm feeling sad,
Violet is for when I'm feeling bad,
Red is for the anger I have inside,
White is for when I'm terrified,
Green with envy,
That means jealousy,
Dark pink is for when I am in love,
Yellow is the joy I'm dreaming of.

Concerned for you,
Concerned for me,
Just think of why we are happy.

Magenta is for when I'm feeling hurt,
Indigo is for when I'm feeling cursed,
Turquoise is for when I'm feeling sick,
Gold is for when I'm feeling lit,
Silver is for when I shine like a star,
Either from the moon or secretly from afar.
Concerned for you,
Concerned for me,
Just think of why we are happy!

Lexi Ross (11)
The William Allitt School, Newhall

THE FUTURE

In the future, there will be flying cars, like 'Back to the Future'
Some will be grey, some will be green
Some will definitely not be seen
In the future, there will be no roads, no limits
Flatpack houses from Ikea, could this become a future idea?
In the future, there will be jetpacks that are twice the speed of flying cars,
They will take you far from Earth and far among the stars
In the future, we will live on Mars, there will be no cars
We will live in a remote dome with unlimited supplies
We could teleport from planet to planet,
there will be no planes
In the future, everything is possible

Jacob Paul Ratcliffe (11)
The William Allitt School, Newhall

ADVENTURE

A nd every step I take, my spine begins to shiver
D eathly creaking floorboards, my hands begin to quiver
V ery slowly, I'll walk to not wake up the monster, and
E nd up in its stomach, that means I definitely disturbed its slumber
N ow I hear groaning and whining, he's definitely awake!
T ime to go hide, run and duck to get away,
U nder the table, I'm definitely going to stay!
R ipped it off the big monster did, then he left, honestly it was quite quick
E nded up getting a treat, from the monster who I call my brother.

Mikey Wilkinson (11)
The William Allitt School, Newhall

DREAMS

Gazing at the sunset,
Wondering where I am,
Am I in a field?
I'm lost and afraid,
The birds flying past,
Continuing for days,
The colours in the sky,
Brings out your eyes,
Your pointy horn passing by,
The teal mane floating in the wind,
I know where I am,
A mythical land,
As I scramble through the ground,
I discovered something, not land,
But a crystal clear pond,
Showing my face,
I close my eyes,
Taking a deep breath,
Opening them again, I wonder,
Where am I?
I am in bed,
It was all a dream,
Or was it real?

Keeley Wood (11)
The William Allitt School, Newhall

THE FEAR OF BEING ALONE

When fear kicks in,
And your eyes well up,
You know it's that time,
Fear has suddenly struck,
You get this weird feeling,
A feeling like no other,
It hits you so bad,
You just can't help but shudder,
The feeling is so strong,
Your heart starts racing,
You walk around the room,
But you can't stop yourself from pacing,
You have a stress meltdown,
It is very scary for you,
You wait ever so patiently,
Till all is good as new.

Erin Marie Satchwell (12)
The William Allitt School, Newhall

THE FUTURE IS DEAD

T he future is dead
H owever hard it seems to face
E very minute, every hour is one we should chase

F or millions of years, there have been many predictions
U ntil this day we have made non-fiction,
T hat there will be a day where,
U p in space, an asteroid will form
R ight in line with the Earth's wall.
E ventually, it will hit, and you will hear a noise that will break you into tears.

Natalie Ruddle (11)
The William Allitt School, Newhall

FUTURE INVENTIONS

With future inventions, I could fly,
Across several nations, it would be mine.
I'd have so much power, all in my grasp,
Maybe a time machine, it'll make people gasp!
They said it's impossible. For me, it's a no,
People said I was silly, not with all that I know.
With future inventions, I could fly,
Across several nations, it would be mine.

George Spencer (11)
The William Allitt School, Newhall

ROBOTS

There once was a robot called Bon,
And the boy who owned him was called John.
They danced and pranced and galloped all day,
Until Bon just finally broke.
John cried and cried and cried all day,
Until he went online,
And when he saw Steve,
It was like Christmas Eve,
And they both lived happily ever after.

Peter Robson (11)
The William Allitt School, Newhall

CREEPY CITY

I was playing with my friends, then wandered off a bit,
I saw a dark city and took a look,
All I saw were shops,
It's like the city was dead,
I thought I must be dreaming,
It's all in my head,
I had no phone,
To contact home,
I didn't know my way back,
Oh no, I've lost my way home!

Libby Fearn (11)
The William Allitt School, Newhall

THE FUTURE

Welcome aboard our polluted Earth
The end is awfully near
Smoke rises from the deep,
dark ground
Atomic power takes over our land
Nuclear bombs are easily formed
The light of day you will not see
You won't survive a day
Everyone would love to get away
Say goodbye to our polluted Earth.

Emily Mae Brookes (11)
The William Allitt School, Newhall

THE MOAN

All on my own
Alone in the world
No one can hear me
I can just hear a moan
I want to know what it could be
Let's find out, they could be here to save me
Maybe it's a prince, maybe it's a knight
Or it's just an owl hooting in the sky.

Franki Sweet (11)
The William Allitt School, Newhall

A POEM ABOUT HURRICANES

The hurricane stormed across the country,
Twisting and turning, backwards and forwards.
Causing destruction and devastation everywhere,
People who see are in despair.
They all do really care,
Residents want to move but... where?

Skye Evans-Sellers (11)
The William Allitt School, Newhall

THE FUTURE

Nobody knows what it's like
All you can do is guess
If I could choose what the future
would be about
this is what I would guess
Flying cars, hoverboards
and high tech homes
If you could guess what it's like
you might not guess right
or get to see if you were right
but the future isn't easy to guess
even if you know what's next
If you're a kid who can travel
in time and not lose your mind
then you can come back to your kind
and tell them what it's like
from robots to hover cars
to hoverboards galore
Will the old, human life be no more?
Only the future can say more
even if it's tomorrow or the week after
the future cannot be told unless you're from it
and know what is told
not many people know if flying cars
and hoverboards will even exist
Even if you're in it, you're there to win.

Kia Ann Cooke (13)
Tudor Grange Samworth Academy, Leicester

THE SHADOW

In the sunlight it stalks me,
It's repeating my steps.
You may think it's normal...
But the creepier it gets

It's normal to see it in the day on the road
But strange seeing its outlines on the dark wall
Its white eyes flicker
They're wide and bright
They're staring at me in the middle of the night

I'm awake under the covers of my bed
hoping that I won't end up dead
Every now and again I take a peak
It's spreading around my room like black ink
I find its face in the dark corner
Will this nightmare take any longer?

It's pacing around me,
like a hungry vulture.
it grins viciously,
what is this evil creature?

I sit up in a panic,
was this really all a dream?
The shadow's nowhere near me,
but I still don't think I'm free...
I have this nasty feeling

It still gives me the chills
I feel that someone's watching...
Waiting for the kill...

Hanna Maria Szlaga (13)
Tudor Grange Samworth Academy, Leicester

THE FUTURE

The year is 3018
It's 1000 years in the future
There are flying cars
which eat energy bars
Everywhere there are skyscrapers
which are high in the sky
There are no trees
this is what happens when you build
What else is missing?
Oil, which has been wasted
Buses go to different places
You can go to Mars
I mean the planet, not the chocolate bars

Do you want to go to the Antarctic?
Tough, you can't
All the ice has melted
just because of air pollution
The rivers on Mars flow
The wind on Mars blows
The stars near Mars glow
The cars on Mars are slow
so are the chocolate bar sales

The wars have stopped
The years of peace haven't
The world is tough

But this isn't enough
This is the future.

Ben Lunn (13)
Tudor Grange Samworth Academy, Leicester

CHRISTMAS WISH

The day has come,
I walk down the stairs,
The tree is up,
All I see is green and red,
This year, I'm fifteen,
the year to become an adult,
the year for no more dolls,
it's the year for money,
I see presents under the tree of magic,
big, small and medium,
I silently creep to the kitchen,
there I see food,
chicken, veg and mash, the yummy ones come first,
I walk back into the living room,
and that's where she stood,
my big sister is back,
I ran up to her to give her a hug,
that's what I was about to cry,
and then shouted to mum,
that's when she came running in
My Christmas wish has finally come true,
Today, I feel blessed.

Cassidy Katie McKinnon (14)
Tudor Grange Samworth Academy, Leicester

AN ODE TO FOOTBALL

Everything I ever dreamed of since I was a little kid
the passion, drama, enthusiasm
it's all just amazing
no wonder it's called the beautiful game
It runs through the family
my dad wasn't bad either
fulfilled his dreams
played the game with such respect and love
well, to follow his footsteps will be pretty tough
Especially when he's playing with the like of:
George Best, Bobby Moore, and the great Zinedine Zidane
that's a big, big ask
For me, I just want to be the best I can be
strive for new levels and aim for my goals
take the opportunity by the scruff of the neck
just believe you can do it
take your chance
#takeyourchance!

Hassan Ismail
Tudor Grange Samworth Academy, Leicester

BREATHING

I manage to cry
I feel short, not tall
I get that feeling
That this life isn't mine
That I can't control
That everyone is living
And I'm just
Breathing
Watching and waiting
For what?
Drowning them
Grinding into pieces
So that I can blow them away
Like leaves in the air
But the system is broken
They are melting
Melting gently like ice
Flashback depression
anxiety and yet
nobody
listens to me
So I was taught not to show emotions or feelings
at least, not in the cold light of day
Being overwhelmed is hard
They're pulling me down
They are dark.

Nicol Slizewska-Gniazdowska (13)
Tudor Grange Samworth Academy, Leicester

NEW ADVENTURE

Adventure to my new school,
all I can see is how tall the walls are,
all I can hear are little kids,
all I can feel is my heart racing
bouncing out of my chest.

It all seems so scary on your first day
not knowing who anyone is,
nor what they think.

Missing all my old friends
remembering all my memories,
making new ones. Trying to fit in.
Building my confidence.

Meeting new teachers, meeting new people.
New rules, new ways, new clothes,
it all seems so real.

What if I get bullied?
Maybe no one will like me?

I'll have to find out, I say.

Alivia Hay
Tudor Grange Samworth Academy, Leicester

INNER FEELINGS

The storm was dwelling up inside of me
I needed to let it out; I needed a key
There was desperation in my eyes
The people around me were full of lies

Didn't know what to believe
It was like a conspiracy, against me
Too much for me to handle
It was not time... to blow out the candle

The darkness around me was now fading
The gloomy clouds above me were finally separating
My path was now clear
I no longer needed to live in fear

I knew what I had to do
All I needed was a clue
A clue that led me to the real culprit
To prove that I didn't do it...

Aprinder Kaur (13)
Tudor Grange Samworth Academy, Leicester

THE FUTURE

The year is 3069,
It has been 1051 years since diesel cars were used,
There are only flying cars that run on electricity,
Everywhere there are floating buildings,
Held up by the old bullet shellings,
There is no longer war,
There is no longer crime.

The trees and plants still grow,
On this planet, we all know,
The population we all know,
The population goes very slow,
The cats all flow,
The light pollution does not grow.

The bright stars,
Near Mars,
Rule the cars,
That eat electricity bars,
Old celebrities are now amongst the stars.

Mason Thomas
Tudor Grange Samworth Academy, Leicester

HAIKU POETRY

I go to the shop
There I buy a bubble dress
I'm happy at home

It is my party
I go to buy food and juice
It is so funny

I draw a flower
This flower has two colours
It's so beautiful

I have a good friend
In the night she slept at mine
Tomorrow is school

I go to parties
The party at Ally's house
I have energy

I'm in English hour
So I write a lot for it
Now finished lesson

In Romania
Now I'm in England for school
I start in school soon.

Cristina Maria Jipa (12)
Tudor Grange Samworth Academy, Leicester

WINDOWS TO THE SOUL

He broke her heart,
They couldn't stand being apart,
She couldn't stand the pain,
It burned like a flame,
She cried until nothing more came out,
Every single feeling she had was doubt,
She didn't want it to end like this,
She missed the feeling of his lips,
She had no role or part to play,
She didn't have anything to say,
The teardrops ran off her nose,
She cried in corners where nobody goes,
Her smile is fake, a goddess of disguise,
Trust me, you can see it, just look in her eyes.

Emma Foxon (13)
Tudor Grange Samworth Academy, Leicester

A FEW P SHORT

Finally, here I am at my destination
the grocery store to be exact
I need to hurry up and get what I want
because from the outside it looks packed
all I need is to get myself a packet of sweets
Here I am at the sweet, sugary aisle
I can't find the sweets I'm looking for
this may take a while
in the corner of my eye
I see a bright red pack
Yes! Here they are, I've been looking for that
Walking to the cashier with the thing that I need
Please don't be over £1.00, I beg and I plead!

Nicole Szalai
Tudor Grange Samworth Academy, Leicester

INNER FEELINGS

Your eyes sparkle like the sun,
I like how you tie your hair in a bun,
I love the way you walk and talk,

Without you, I don't know how different my life would be,
I know we haven't been together for too long,
and I know we won't last forever

but for now, let's try to make it last a lifetime,
but I love you and I hope you love me too!

I know we haven't known each other for long,
but I know we had a very special connection,
that makes me passionate about you!

Cyrus Marriott (12)
Tudor Grange Samworth Academy, Leicester

DEPRESSION POEM

I feel lonely and abandoned, it's true
although it gets covered up with happiness and goodness outside
I may as well be the colour blue,
I always punish myself and might even try to hide
from all things bad that'll be out there lurking, waiting,
probably ready for me to come out, that wouldn't be a surprise.
People try to make me happy and stay like that
even though sometimes it works and happiness fills me,
I still truly feel like a kind rat,
who never talks and loves cups of tea.

Eleanor Chambers (12)
Tudor Grange Samworth Academy, Leicester

ADVENTURE FEELINGS ABOUT AN ADVENTURE IN A RAINFOREST

The leaves touch my smooth, silky skin
The smell of plants and flowers hits my nose
tall grass tickling my legs slowly
the tall trees swish in the soft wind
like a film with the sound effects on

I would rather stay here than home
Creaking, the wood snaps, *snap!*
I start to worry it's on my feet
"Ouch, ouch..." I say
I pull my feet away
and walk away, relieved

My feet are starting to ache in agony
I carry on my journey.

Stefani Todorovic
Tudor Grange Samworth Academy, Leicester

IF I WERE LONELY

If I were an animal who would I be?
Just read the poem, you will see,
If I were an elephant
I'd swing my trunk with glee,
If I were a hippo
I would eat, eat, eat!
If I were an eagle
I would stalk my prey, night or day,
If I were a lion, I'd be king!
If I were a sloth, I'd be in a zoo
sitting in a tree with the local bees, (hello!)
If I were me, I'd stay me
because we are all unique
no matter what anyone says
believe in yourself!

Cole Barratt (12)
Tudor Grange Samworth Academy, Leicester

HAIKU POETRY

Haiku poetry

I got my breakfast
It tasted like vanilla
I'm happy I ate

I left out for school
I went to school and sat down
My school day ended

I went home and changed
I went to chill in my room
I ate my dinner

A new day started
I had snacks and went to school
Then the day ended

Then I went back home
I got ready to go out
I went back to home

I ate my dinner
I went to my room to sleep
Fell asleep at last.

Shay Tramaine Dixon (12)
Tudor Grange Samworth Academy, Leicester

ABOVE

And I was lost, lost in the dark
Without escape being apart
From all the things that I had loved
Trying to be again above

Above the limits, above the sky
To have one chance, to try and try
To find the way back to your heart
And to forget that we're apart

Every time you ask, I pretend I'm fine
Even if I know what's going on in my mind

Even if I try to forget you, I can't
'Cause I keep you always, here in my heart.

Florentina Denisia Murat (13)
Tudor Grange Samworth Academy, Leicester

FUTURE

The sky is dark and lights shine
as people drive their flying cars
in the brightly lit city

Shopping is as easy as one click
and all your items will be delivered

But that is what we hoped
as World War III began
so all is lost because of us
if only we could go back now
then this would not have happened here

As World War III ends
and all that we hoped came back to us
and we built our dreams
and we lived our lives.

Deividas Zemlauskis (12)
Tudor Grange Samworth Academy, Leicester

ALL ABOUT THE SPORT

Football has always been great
especially with your mate
Smashing that ball into the net
Before you know it, you've got a private jet

Boxing has always been a punch
You've never got time to hunch
On Saturday, I hope Joshua wins by knockout
It'll obviously be an extremely tough bout

Basketball has always been a throw
But you cannot stop and go
Dribbling is obviously allowed
also, it is not that hard to be fouled.

Abube Calvin Onuchukwu (13)
Tudor Grange Samworth Academy, Leicester

ODE TO SNOW

The whitest thing ever,
It is boring, never,
As children play,
They're gone all day,
Playing in the snow.

There's lots going away,
Playing for the day,
There's plenty of drinks,
When boilers are on the blink,
As to get heat, arms are linked.

When it's time to go,
We say goodbye to snow,
As the heat melts it away,
Children carry on with their day,
No more playing in the snow.

Dylan Wardle
Tudor Grange Samworth Academy, Leicester

MY FUTURE

In the future, I will become a sporty athlete
breaking all the records in the history books
and the fastest man in the world
setting records that will never be broken
whilst that's happening I'll have my children starting school
and having an education
and then hopefully a family of athletes who make it to the top
and be in the papers or television
"The most famous family in the world," the reporter would say.

Augustine Jakopo-Taylor (12)
Tudor Grange Samworth Academy, Leicester

THE FOX

I looked over my shoulder and saw an orange-furred fox,
I saw the fox's eyes staring at a box,
The box was brown and dull,
Opposite the box was a bull,
Inside of the box, a twang was heard,
A rabbit leapt out and it was spared,
The fox ran away, deeper into the forest,
The bull sprinted towards a florist.
The florist got broken down,
A little girl picked up some flowers shaped like a crown.

Ethan Thomas
Tudor Grange Samworth Academy, Leicester

INNER FEELINGS

Life is not perfect, as all of us know
And sometimes we might have to solve things on our own
We all have our struggles and hardships
We all have our ups and downs
We all might at some point feel depressed
And that there is no way to find success
But what we can do is find an escape
Discover a passion, something that you like
To make you feel good, bring you back to life.

Alexandra Brinzoi (13)
Tudor Grange Samworth Academy, Leicester

ADVENTURE

I legged it to the shops
with what felt like a grand
I would buy nothing bland
or my nan would faint and the only cure would be
a sniff of paint
I ran around the aisle where I found my treats
There was a bag of sweets
I bought two, nothing more or I would be poor
I ran home, slung my bag
I floated upstairs as I turned on my console.

Anthony William Shelley (13)
Tudor Grange Samworth Academy, Leicester

RHYMING COUPLETS

Last year I got bitten by a shark
He played it very sneaky, as it was very dark
I didn't even see it coming
Well, maybe it was because I wasn't even looking

Now I can't complain
As I have no more to explain
At least I am back out of the water
Now I am ready to not be part of a mass slaughter.

Corey Beatty
Tudor Grange Samworth Academy, Leicester

TRUTH HURTS

Imagine looking at yourself in bed
the thought of yourself being dead
that's how they feel but without a bed

All day long their hands are empty
they beg and they beg but they won't lend a penny
as dark as it seems, it's just the truth
and as they say, 'truth hurts.'

Abbas Jafari (12)
Tudor Grange Samworth Academy, Leicester

THE FUTURE

In the future I want to fly very high in the sky,
I want the cars to take you far, some places
you can't go in life
to Narnia or in the sky
around the world one hundred times
for everything to be free
just like I want to be
for everything that is extinct to be alive again.

Holly Harding
Tudor Grange Samworth Academy, Leicester

WEEKEND

Friday, Friday, the day you celebrate for
finishing school and a day for you to flourish
with friends and family
you run and fall as your dreams never end

Saturday, the day you relax in bed
with a smile as you sleep until
10am or 9am
for no one shall wake you up.

Mohammad Ahmadi
Tudor Grange Samworth Academy, Leicester

ODE

It is big and grand
It makes a magnificent sound
My fingers run up and down the keys
They bounce around with their own mind

You can play any tune
There are nine grades you can do
You can finally feel alive
with the grand piano tune.

Cody Watson (13)
Tudor Grange Samworth Academy, Leicester

TODAY

Haiku poetry

I'm going to school
I met my friend on the way
We spoke about slime

We made it to school
We went to our lesson... why?
Friend went home early

I went to a club
Then came home to a cute dog
sat waiting for me.

Chelsey Smullen
Tudor Grange Samworth Academy, Leicester

THE FUTURE

Haiku poetry

The future is here
the robot cars are flying
I love it so much

Cars drive me to school
every day they also take
me to McDonald's

They can let you drive
but with a safety system
The future is cool.

Kane Donovan (12)
Tudor Grange Samworth Academy, Leicester

MIND FULL

Thoughts swirling around me
Piling more and more into my brain
overloading myself with ideas
that the only thing here is pain

They collide with each other aggressively
'You're not good enough', 'You're like the rest.'
But I put these thoughts away
Locking the key and going to bed

But when I open my eyes again
the thoughts flood back into my brain
I feel sad and useless and lonely
So I close my eyes and there I lie

Pain, pain, and more pain
that's the only thing I can think about now
as I sit on the ground shaking
hugging my knees and feeling foul

My mind is full of ideas
that take over me throughout the day
this is a teenager's mind
and trust me, it's here to stay.

Amélie Tuck (13)
Wilsthorpe School, Long Eaton

HER MIND

Sometimes I struggle to get through to her,
Sometimes I struggle to tell her the right thing,
Even though she knows I'm right,
I am constantly shut out.

Sometimes she has these crazy ideas,
And it's my job to tell her it's not healthy,
But she's just so good at shutting me down,
So she carries on and ignores me anyway.

We both know that she knows,
She knows that I'm always here,
She knows that what I'm saying is right,
Yet, still, every day I am contradicted.

Sometimes I wish she'd just listen,
I know it would be better for both of us,
When I tell her to put her phone down or go outside,
She should do it, I know she'll feel better.

She likes to shut herself away,
She thinks her phone will make her happier,
I tell her to talk to her family,
But she believes they'll just bore her.

Some days she cries for so long,
And I'm screaming at her to smile,

I want her to know that she's perfect,
But she never seems to hear me.

One day, I know I'll get through to her,
One day, I know she'll realise,
That all along I've been right,
And the battle with her mind will be over.

Izzy Johnson (13)
Wilsthorpe School, Long Eaton

Young Writers Information

We hope you have enjoyed reading this book – and that you will continue to in the coming years.

If you're a young writer who enjoys reading and creative writing, or the parent of an enthusiastic poet or story writer, do visit our website **www.youngwriters.co.uk**. Here you will find free competitions, workshops and games, as well as recommended reads, a poetry glossary and our blog. There's lots to keep budding writers motivated to write!

If you would like to order further copies of this book, or any of our other titles, then please give us a call or visit **www.youngwriters.co.uk**.

Young Writers
Remus House
Coltsfoot Drive
Peterborough
PE2 9BF
(01733) 890066
info@youngwriters.co.uk

Join in the conversation!
Tips, news, giveaways and much more!

f YoungWritersUK   🐦 @YoungWritersCW